More Praise for *To Eve*

To Eve is a luminous book-length poem dedicated to Sarah Dickenson Snyder's infant granddaughter, Eleanor Virginia Edwards – EVE and written in devotion to the feminine spirit which precedes all beginnings. Moving in tender and urgent inquiry, the poem asks timeless, elemental questions *"Where were you before you were born?"* In dialogue with Eve – child, ancestor, and original mother – Snyder inhabits the weightlessness of origins, tracing a path "under the skin / of the small history you lived in." Fierce and soft by turns, *To Eve* carries the reader through a richly emotional landscape where feathered imagery rises from the marrow of the poem itself. This work is a meditation on the enduring presence of the feminine – an offering meant not only for one child, but for all who read.
— **Christine Bess Jones**, author of *Limb of Water* and *Now Calls Me Daughter*

In a lush love letter *To Eve*, Sarah Dickenson Snyder imagines ashared experience of motherhood with this archetypal womanand speaks to her directly: *I give you this splintered, luminous world / you left me.* The lyrical movement of the poet's mind invites readers to flow with both her own considerations and the mythic Eve's – life and loss, presence and absence, reality and memory. Dickenson Snyder uses form beautifully to contain wonder and hold space. With reverence for the unblemished perfection of new life and for natural flora and fauna – *every tree humming with wind and bird sound* – the speaker deeply embodies the experience of living in tune with the natural worldwhile recognizing its fullness with the eyes of daughter, mother, and grandmother. "I'm coming," she says, on the way to meet her granddaughter, *my arms ready / for the heavy head of a sleeping baby.* This is a book-length poem that will hold you in truth and beauty.
— **Melissa McInstry**, winner of a 2026 Pushcart Prize

TO EVE
A BOOK LENGTH POEM

SARAH DICKENSON SNYDER

Nixes Mate Books
Allston, Massachusetts

Copyright © 2026 Sarah Dickenson Snyder

Book design by d'Entremont
Cover image used with permission.

All rights reserved. This book or any portion thereof may not be reproduced or used in any manner whatsoever without the express written permission of the publisher except for the use of brief quotations in a book review or scholarly journal.

ISBN 978-1-949279-64-1

Nixes Mate Books
POBox 1179
Allston, MA 02134
nixesmate.pub

For all the curious, loving, funny, smart, and resilient women who have held, inspired, shaped, forgiven, and strengthened me, especially the newest arrival on our miraculous, spinning planet – my granddaughter, Eleanor Virginia Edwards (EVE)

With gratitude to these publications in which various parts of this book-length poem, sometimes in different iterations, first appeared:

3Element Review, 433 Journal, Birdcoat Quarterly, Catamaran Literary Journal, Dear O Deer, Dreich Magazine, Ekphrastic Review, Exist Otherwise Literary Journal, Funicular Magazine, Gyroscope Review, Kosmos Quarterly, Lake Journal, Lunch Ticket, On the Seawall, One Art, One Sentence Poems, The Orchards Poetry Review, PoemTown, Ponder Review, Presence Journal, Quartet Journal, Ruminate, Second Coming, Silver Birch Press, Sky Island Journal, Smartish Pace, South Florida Poetry Journal, Stonecoast Review, Synkroniciti, Third Wednesday Magazine, Writing in a Woman's Voice, & *TAB: The Journal of Poetry and Poetics*

TO EVE

There was a story
in *rib, snake, & apple,*
but sometimes you need to
say *frost* to statue the world
so you can find what is lost.

Or even *sand* to feel your feet
sink, enter what is below.

Don't be afraid of darkness.
It is there that we are solved,
our hinge to gods. Everywhere
we can't see, there.

The way pollen enters
even closed windows,

the way fingertips
sweep skin and find

the dust of all
the other worlds.

It must have been hard to be the beginning   the one pulled

from a cage of ribs without the sweet smell of milk

or symbiosis of skin, that's probably why you and he began your cleaving,

arriving already long-limbed & flat bellied.

The only sanity would be to sleep next to him,

to reach & find spaces in your darknesses under the stars.

Both of you   motherless.

I can see you wandering on the spongy soil where there's too much to harvest,

every tree humming with wind & bird sound.   Ferns generous.

And those leafy walls of scent: lilac, jasmine & their shadows.

All the furred & winged animals seem indifferent & ornamental.

Did you count the loud crows without numbers? Follow their spiriting from branch to sky

& beyond to the changing moon, barely there in blueness?

You were surrounded & uncertain.   A world where a seed begets tree,

a tree its fruit. Every stone in a perfect place except the small, smooth ones

you might pick up. Is this when you spoke?

Maker, the next time you want to make yourself into flesh & blood,

place us in a mother, let us

collapse into her arms & know birth.

Did you listen for a voice
to turn toward,

a sound that meant *I am*

*the heartbeat you once knew
as every cell of you grew.*
A soft whale song

(or the gentled water
around octopus arms)
in long grasses, the horizon

more green, more trees
& clear sky.
How you wandered,

never imagined
yourselves once
fed by a breast.

At first, no rules. Just live
in the light the Maker created
& sleep in the darkness,
animals flying or crawling
or sliding through the long grasses.

Never a child,
never untamable,
never skipped in the dust
with others, only the lushness,
& sitting on a rock that holds

the warmth of a close star.

Did you touch
the snake, the one
that waited?

Did it speak to you
or did you just want
to hear another voice?

You were naked.
Adam was dressed in shadow.
The snake escaped its skin.

Past the shaggy fabric of willows,
past the crow constellation
dotting the meadow
to branches reaching
into the unflawed, blank sky,
did you notice ripeness?

Not this.

Think wind,
its sudden roar,
its touch beyond
the flash of sound.

You understood instructions,
but planted inside you was a little fist
that wanted what it wanted.
Did the Maker say you could not fly?

Well, then your dreams
became feathered.

from the beginning
a woman tastes
unlids the box
nobody will open
of course she must
she is the skin
that says kiss me
so life can start
she is surrender
& courage
the wetlands
& cliff edge

Everything starts with you,
with a feeling of being pulled
by invisible string.
All the shadows of mothers
reach back to your hunger,
your banishment, the birth
of your sons, how one
killed the other,
all the long years you lived,
nothing sad scrubbed away,
your first part a marionette
made of a rib bone,
then your hand reaching
for what shined in the sun.

The way I touch the moss
that has a sign *Keep Off!*

how I made love
with the one man
I would marry
on that mossy patch
by the river after
everyone had left.

Where did you find
your soul?

Maybe in the marrow
of your bones, that first

rib taken for you.
You did hear other voices –

from above,
the one sounding like wind

or thunder. Then the softness
of Adam's, that small knot

moving inside his throat,
a voice like rain song

so different from the winged
landing on branches or the hush

of the snake. Your soul
sounded full

of certainty. Remember?
It said only, *Fill yourself.*

Nothing more.

I bet you licked your teeth clean
with a tinge of release
& dissolve, a finishing
in that small molecule
of being satisfied.
Don't be afraid, Adam said,
but you were already spinning
with a weightlessness
finding a way
under the skin
of the small history you lived in,
the touch of leaf & wind,
now cold & somehow hollow
after the swallowing.

Fear rolling over a voice can eclipse
the truth. Some of us find the way back
by expanding our ribs as you did.
How you cleared your clouded

throat, opened your mouth, & spoke.
You saw no apparitions, of course.
There were no spirits yet, only raccoons,
wolves, the feathered in your world,
that rock where you sat & decided.
The smoothness of its surface –
it could be a museum piece:

> *Here is where the first woman*
> *watched a world unfold*
> *& became hungry.*

You were fire

or maybe on fire

or maybe your tongue fiery

                                        all the world succulent

            & poised to be eaten.

You were hungry

for more.

Maybe to dwarf the growth
of what the Maker wanted to control,
the Maker should have started earlier.

You sensed the sea,
the iridescence
in the underneath of a shell.

Did you know

you *wanted* to go...

A burning on your fingertips,
on your lips as if *you'd* been bitten.

Would there be fireflies,
would the lupines bloom
there? How the green leaves
waited, & in-one-wet-night
the clustered purple stalks
emerged.

Was endless a kind of paradise
or did you admit you were bored?

That was the sin.

A line of regal turkeys
crossed the meadow.
& there a doe,
her young fawn & its tinny cry
a rippling.

Are you ready? Adam asked.
You stood,

took nothing
except a small piece
of the tree in your palm.

Did you miss it?
Nothing underripe,
no ice sheets or sirens,
no shekels, no texts –
a sleepy, quiet greenness
with peacocks & eagles
& hanging mangoes,
everything still
& shadow-flecked
again & again.

        Or had you left the *loneliest* place?

                Do you know about the cherubim
                & the flaming sword –
                the new sentry
                around that apple tree?

You walked east
toward homecoming
to bear children
where fruit was not forbidden
& snakes were footless.

You squeezed your fist,
the tiny sharpness
still there.

Breathe the new sky,
everything woven in.

In the desert night
you saw people & animals
& other things above.
Back in the garden the faces
in the shadows of leafy branches,
eyes & smiles
in the whorled bark of trees,
small teeth in the petals
of a daisy, something known.

Now surrounded
by darkness & stars,
you said, *Do you see that?*
pointing up & tracing lines
to connect each brightness,
outlining a ladle like the one
he carved & left behind.

He whispered, *Yes*
& turned toward you.

After, there was no fear,
no snake, no shame.

You stayed awake
& named what was revealed
in the spaces the stars make:
dipper, wolf, arrow, sister.

Unprotected
on the high smooth rocks
you breathed sun.
Your feet hardened
covered with leathery leaves
sewn together by the bone needles
you'd fashioned & uncoiled twine,
sensing the cusp of not being.
Each rock named – *mica, jasper,
sandstone.* The world banked
by mountains or clouds,
Everywhere wind & sun.
Was the Maker there? Ever?

How you knew
what lips were meant to do.

That surge where every cell needs
to touch every other cell.

All that wouldn't have happened
if you hadn't asked him to kiss you,

if you weren't
hungry?

I doubt you ate meat.
You'd prefer to touch the softness
of a cow's hide, sink into
those large, dark eyes.

Your first blood was your own.
The Maker placed in you what you never
emerged from: fallopian tubes & a womb.

In the cool heaven of evening,
did the Maker speak to you.
All those tiny pieces of light

& one moon flung in blackness
before the forbidding.
Now borders uncrossable

& fertile lands you must find.
No more words from the Maker.
No more, *Follow*.

What about a wax-sealed letter? A voice
decipherable. Your world edged
with thunder & turbulence in the firmament.

Your skin weathered, still hungry.
You moved through the muddied riverbeds,
plucked mushrooms, unearthed wild onions.

You ate what grew from the soil,
picked up a stone, a smooth heaviness
to hold. When you rested, you found a stick,

drew spirals in the clay or sand,
messages to no one. This was
the beginning. You read the trees.

You heard the rain for the first time
in the many sways from dark to light,
that muffled drumming against the pine boughs
you placed above. A world waiting
to pull water from the sky.
You knew about the ground,
but the sky belongs to the flighted.
Water washes away caution.
How did you learn to swim
in the deep pools in the garden?
Would you ever learn to fly?

You thought of the snake,
wondered if what was between you
was kinship or imagination,
was it a voice or just another you
inside of you? Did the snake yearn
for legs? Maybe someday
you will love the snake.

Someday you will find a home
& stay. A garden will grow,
a row of three trees.

You moved as if you were escaping
a trembling past
not a flowering garden.

Your bodies gave warmth
to the darkness. One night
you found a carpeted pine needle bed,

the softest yet. You dreamed of an endless sea,
described the smell of salt to him
& the blurred world below,

that galaxy of shell, kelp, & fish.
He stared at you like you was the origin
of things unseen. Sometimes he leads you

over the sandstone of a windswept canyon,
his hand reaching back for yours.
In this unabandoned land

You search for shades of green.
The sky spills another story.
Something unmistakable

grows inside you, changing
the skin of your belly, you now
rounded, like a chestnut.

A request delivered,
a restarting
pressing into you.

One must close
her eyes
to see herself
in the roar
of waterfalls.
One must be framed
in the darkness
of small
to repair.
You are not
the skyscraper
or the redwood,
no, you are one
brick, the foundation,
the centering,
the seed,
you need
closed eyes
to see
your obedience
to gravity,
to yourself.

Did chipmunk or swallow follow you,
darting or diving into the space you left behind?

Maybe we all have some small dot
in the middle of concentric circles,
willing us to stretch the skin's tautness
over our bones & let go, an arc
of us skimming through air,
seeking a landing deep
into the center
of another.

There is a small ferry.
Not the kind with wings,
but the one with a soft,
puttering motor
to take us beyond
what we know.

You liked seeing him
from afar,
his slim body
returning to you
with an armful
of what had fallen
for you.

*Let us know how
to have another*, you
said to no one.

We are born from a mother.
And we also die.

birth and hunger and love and death and
birth and hunger and love and death and
birth and hunger and love and death and
birth and hunger and love and death and
birth and hunger and love and death and
birth and hunger and love and death and
birth and hunger and love and death and
birth and hunger and love and death and
birth and hunger and love and death and
birth and hunger and love and death and
birth and hunger and love and death and
birth and hunger and love and death and
birth and hunger and love and death and
birth and hunger and love and death and
birth and hunger and love and death and
birth and hunger and love and death and
birth and hunger and love and death and
birth and hunger and love and death and
birth and hunger and love and death and
birth and hunger and love and death and
birth and hunger and love and death and
birth and hunger and love and death and
birth and hunger and love and death and
birth and hunger and love and death and
birth and hunger and love and death and
birth and hunger and love and death and
birth and hunger and love and death and
birth and hunger and love and death and
birth and hunger and love and death and
birth and hunger and love and death and

(There I was
making a basket
with the hem
of my T-shirt pulled up
to carry the fallen apples.

& then
a distance
shortened.

I'll tell you what
I don't remember –

something fell
out of me
when I found out
we all leave.

What was carefree
dropped its shiny seeds
into the sad
of not-forever.

A loneliness,
this anguish –

like moving through
a wideness of air
wingless.)

When I first realized
that humans die,

she never said, *In the darkness
you will find yourself —*

be open to every small fire in you
to calm my dread.

When I didn't know the arc of my life,
Grow something loved & tender.

Nor the uncovering
of what she saw in me:

*You are weather-shaped,
listen to the wind.*

Unmothered, you implored the Maker
in the garden to let go of clay & rib
& plant within your womb the first child.

Once the quickening, you cared for another
more than for yourself. Every mother swells.

But no word can contain all that.

How could you have known that what emerged
from the muck & blood of you, that first son
from within you would kill, that the first son you loved
would cause the first death.

Death should have entered like this:
first Adam, then you, then Cain, then Abel.

Death at old age, we expect.

At the funeral a long measure of breaths
among tears & some laughter.

My father bellowed into the microphone
at my mother's service, *What a woman!*
& we all clapped, the texture of a mother
filling the pews. A good dying.

Not like my son's friend, whose casket
he helped carry, the ground slippery
at the gravesite. The sky all gauze
& hurt & wrong.

Abel is gone,
Cain struck him with a stone.

Whiffs of silky scent
ocean & how a body
carries another
The boat
that holds a fragment
at first a tight curl
inside a scribbling
before the forming
of what is born
brought to breath
and named
the one touched
the one spoken to
the fingernails & lashes
& skin that is held
& given milk & sky & sun
a rosy body,
breathable,
readable
placed
in arms next
to breast.
Nothing hidden.
Every pore,
every nerve.
The vessel, the rumble,
a move into mother,
the between
numb or numberless.
No translation.

Both breathing
a separate world.
The first child.

The way he uncurled
from such a small room
untethered & full
of gravity on this ocean
of a mattress in this house –
how can such smallness
have unnested,
no more punctuation
everything running into everything
whose skin is whose
the two buoyed
in a world of air & barrier

a new definition
of hypnosis
you cannot take
your eyes away
from what now lives
outside of you.

Where were you
before you were born?

In my other life,
the purple world.

The mountain's silhouette against
A winter's sky – & there
Venus, its purple wash.

      quagmire   silence

                flames   bone on bone

                a desperate   phone number written on a cocktail napkin

all those gods to curve around, the wild guesses,

the almost-giving-ups, the incisions & the stitches –

                                              to get to this.

Is that you, Eve, come to see
the garden of ferns & lupine
& lilies? Or the raised beds, the way
I pick the outer leaves of each lettuce head?
Have you come to sit with me again?
Mentioned only twice in the Old Testament,
you are a thin thread from the beginning.
How did you recover from one son
killing the other? Do you know
what I say to a god I don't believe in
every night? *Let me die before they do.*
Did you wrap your offerings
around the son who lived?
How did you go on?
All the heaviness
of hold & carry.
You are there, here,
the first mother of us –
you, carbon, & stardust.

Let me tell you about me.

In the land of living & dying, drinking water from a hose, a thickness quenching thirst on a hot & humid afternoon where the air seemed like waves & summer lulled you into thinking you had a lucky life, where fears were caged for the future & all you had to worry about was finding someone in a game of Sardines, where everything could be cured by capturing a flag. Were there a thousand flowers in everyone's garden? Did everyone wear something paisley & white pants only after Memorial Day? & an ice cream truck, can you hear it coming down the crowned road & almost taste the toasted almond popsicle? Another you, another world, but those streets are mapped in your veins, your route home from school through the curly woods past the house your parents almost bought & up the cement steps of 303 East Central Avenue, that sturdy slap of the screen door behind you as you walked into the only home you knew. It's a real Garden of Eden story, the kind where you are exiled from a place you loved & thought was perfect. A house that felt safe, those posters you made from cutting out words & phrases from *Seventeen Magazine* & coming home hungry after field hockey practice to find warm, brown-edged cookies on wax paper, & thirty years later your sister tells you what happened to her there when she was a child.

I came out of the womb, needing
skin & warmth. Probably the first *no*.
My mother was drugged for days

because her father had died
in the hospital as I was born –
where I learned

about wanting.
Life is a steep architecture
of restraint – waiting to reach

for what we want. Eve taught me
about hunger. And her sister, Persephone
who ate six seeds of darkness.

The hardest thing I ever did
was stop bringing a cigarette to my lips.

The smell of cigarettes on my fingers.
When did I tire of stumbling?

My husband and I
have spent the last five months
together in the truck, on a plane,
on a trail, in a bed. I know the map
of his tall, lean body.
How I love his legs,
one of my favorite views
through the rearview mirror
as he pumps the gas.
Is this how Adam & Eve
were day after day,
night after night?

Now he is on a plane without me.
Maybe I made him up from
one of my ribs or a romance novel
I inhaled as a teenager.
No sound of his voice
from another room,
no scent of skin.
I imagine him buckled in.
He'll be polite to the flight attendant
but won't start a conversation.
He'll drift into sleep.
See how I conjure him
when he's not here.
I almost heard his heartbeat
in my ear on his side of the bed
this morning.

Both of us in a stairwell that leads to the parking garage,
we're clinging to each other after watching our son disappear
into a line of backs at security. We won't see him for eight months,
& I am fighting with myself for letting him go,
wondering if he still has a bit of my lipstick on his cheek.
As if that might be enough.

I'm holding the shoe box with my dead cat inside
that my sister lifted from the road & placed in the box
with a pillowcase wrapped around her hands. The only thing
I feel is the emptiness inside my zippered coat
where she used to sleep as I drove in the dark.

I am placing the phone down. My father just told me
the diagnosis, & I know I must go, leave
my two small children with my husband
(I don't know yet that he will make them pancakes
in the shape of their initials). I will fly to the Mayo Clinic
with my dad where they will plant two ports into him,
one in his chest, one in his skull for injecting poison.

I walk into her room where she is
curled in a curve under her comforter,
the floor dotted with crumpled tissues.
Why doesn't anyone want to love me? she asks.

each prayer seeks   safe passage   *from this to that*

                stretches *beyond the face of fear*

                              can we not be here

    without a little fear

        the trapped bat that circles above my bed
          or the lurches on the plane

                      as I dig my fingers in your arm

any sadness
        in our children   the dark of course,

the tall curls of almost crashing waves

                  & high   steep
edges
I turn the fan to high
        so I won't imagine
           a burglar or murderer on the floorboards

below as the house   breathes

it's no wonder
      I feel waist-deep in awake

can't drop the final curtain
        because no one I know has returned
        from death to say, "You'll be fine."

I send out my own blessing:

may fear settle, curl its thin wings
around itself & sleep

How we are
barely clinked into being.

And the tending.

The meager tethering.

And leaving.

No pallbearer list in some drawer.
No certain casket or tombstone.
I won't go happily, but I know
I will go. Those sturdy lupine
& ridiculously yellow daffodils
won't die with me.
That sweet ten-year-old-boy
in the front row could not silence himself
as the actor playing Romeo raised the fake knife
to plunge in his heart.   *She's not really dead!*
he blurted out, his voice a little lightning.
Don't we all want longer stories?
How my son & daughter
will pour my ashes in the pond,
watch a cloud expanding
before erasure or rising.

Speaking of death, it's the last thing
I want, the opposite of hunger,
a language I don't want to learn.

So are there really

three heavens?

The first heaven for

 the nearly drowned,

those who fall into the river,

hit a sunken boulder so hard

an elbow swells into a ball,

& are pulled from the water,

all sputter with something

broken inside, a little box of fear.

The second heaven is for those spinning

upward, the ones more focused on clouds,

the almost winged, who barely need a planet.

The third allows luggage, not the heavy baggage,

the unclaimed treasures found along the way:

smooth stones slipped into a pocket, that charm

always around a neck. Most of what we hold

feels dipped in some mythic river dripping with

water, all of it welcomed, even the birds

we count & those crows we follow.

Does every place with buried ashes
or bones become a church?

Maybe I am letting go
of the fear of death.

Maybe it's the hospice,
the woman I send a writing prompt
to every morning. How different are we?
Death's on her horizon – for me
it's more like a star brightening
in some darknesses.

I feel each vertebra of want
along the inexorable arc
of the living.

Aren't we all in recovery
from the brilliance
of knowing the end
of rib, feather, & leaf?

that covenant I have
with what I cannot see,
what I feel in cupped palms
near the end of a yoga class
when I open my eyes
in the dimmed room
of quiet bodies to see
if the teacher is touching me.
A fistful of invisible, a scarf of it,
the way my hair silvers it.
The truth of what I don't know
for certain, but if I were blindfolded
I might find it after the spinning –
at those early parties,
a papery donkey tail
clutched in my small hand
& me reaching,
reaching for what I hope
is in front of me.

What if
there had been
no garden
no clay
no rib
would we have
made ourselves?
We made children
didn't we?
How easy
that was —
just love
& touch
& my body
a house
a nest
a bloom
a new world full
of yellow leaves
deep rivers
& forgiveness.

You begin to dictate:
"Start *Dear Maker,*
thank you for Your green world,
how thick & perfect
the air there."

Here you are brilliant and alive,
wild under a cloudless sky.
You want to know about
the peonies, the wind,
the swallows, & the owl's night echo.
Do they miss your voice?
Had there been a boat there
or did you just float on the calm water
& wonder at the clouds lying beside you?
What if you had stayed with that
horizon, the colorful fish fins
sculling beneath you?

A half-peck, please, you say to a red-cheeked woman
who palms the bottom of the bag, placing apples
tenderly & saying, *You can fit more in this way.*

The sweetness of fall, the dying season,
the one that you are now a part of –
why is it your favorite?

That need for a few others
to understand. The way I call
one of my sisters,
the theories I share
and let go of or hold on to.
Can you trust *just* Adam?
Sure, what you shared with him
was angel-shaped, but you need
a grown daughter to help you
pick out the perfect dress.

Something comes, even to the abandoned, that last slanted brightness
& the long, precise shadows sealing us to where we are: here.

Broken, yes, filled with vertigo of all we don't know: why-are-we-here-&-what-happens-when-we-die whistling through our chambered bodies.

No mathematics we can memorize. No peace to find
& slip into place. A tumult of unknowing.

I hear the unheard as if my dead mother has taken up residence
in my head, along with my lost father, the grandmother
whose fragrance was a perfume I've never found.

All of them finding a way in. They don't know
about boundaries, don't know to leave the living alone.

We have our own home to straighten, spines to line on the shelves,
a world to fix & cool, unspool the wave of hatred, so much work to do.

I relax my heavy head & hard-working neck
in downward dog, feel the vertebrae under my skin release,
making space inside myself to rename the wind,

imagine my smooth skull, like that Halloween mask I wore once
the elastic strap tight against my hair, sweaty inside. Or that jangle of bones
hanging in the back of a high school science room,

a bulbous head tilting, the sunken sockets empty.
The half-moons below my eyes painted with living
& not sleeping, my mother saying

from her hospital bed, *You look like you have two black eyes.*

Only a few weeks left to live in this world together,
& she finds a way.

The cool grass feels almost wet against my skin.
A summer night breathing stars.
Tell me a story of fragility & how what is given a trellis

will climb toward sky. How time swells & surges spins
willy-nilly in that arsenal of love.

I recite the words that live inside,
the way I had to as a child – what to do in case of fire
or press my palm against my thin chest & spout out

the *Pledge of Allegiance* or after seeing *Jaws* the way my eyes
scanned every glisten in endless water, looking for a fin.

& those first few weeks of being a mother

when I stopped laughing, everything too serious & important
in the atmosphere on the new planet of keeping-someone-alive.

I like that you began with bone – harder than clay, closer to everlasting.
I remember the bits & powder against my fingertips
as I sifted my mother's ashes into the pond,

a murmuration of her in the water,
billowing before settling.

The way when we cover
over the worst, it festers
until we must confess –
how truth-telling
feels like inhaling
after thirsting for air –
to breathe again.
Or for the first time.

A new friend from Afghanistan walks outside
as if to have a conversation with the rain,
her headscarf covering all but her polished face
as she tilts back standing on the wet grass
her eyes open, everything washed over.
Inside, I hold her six-month-old son, Abel,
wonder about the naming, the saving,
the reclaiming. Was she pulled to a return
to when the story started, the first mother losing
& wanting him back. I remember the reaching
for me first, a baby's need to nest a small head
in the warmth of a neck. I remember
starting something over & wanting
to do it better.

I imagine you, Eve
standing in front of *The Weeping Woman.*
The splitting hurts, you lift your hands
& hold your own face, can almost feel
the silvery tears, the edges he's cut,
the world of a woman sliced
into triangles. Are we all gray
inside? & how many sharpened
angles unlived? Red hat with a blue

bow. Packaged grief, you think
as you move closer.
Picasso walls you in, maybe all men
do. A woman weeps, her silenced
eyes haunting or haunted.

Oh, slowed world,
sing to me.

Do palm trees remind you of paradise,
your dearest things pulled back –
the small feather you found
beneath the empty nest,
the pinecone's perfect rows, sharp teeth?
Was there a swing, set on a strong branch?
Let's say there was because you think
you may have had wings once.
you move closer to the water,
love the space right before the curl

of wave crashes. The pause.
Before you reached for fruit.
Before you felt like a fugitive.
You hold your breath.

Is that almost-death,
that shape of waiting for air?
You step over a jellyfish,
know it is dying or dead
beached in the sand,
a cloud of flies settled
on its transparency.
Let the dead sleep.
Immortality would be
tiring, that last quiver
a relief.

& what if

the *Don't...* was swallowed
by wind & all you heard was
...eat from the apple tree

I left fingerprints on silken scarves,
on dangling pomegranates, and the roughness
of a dromedary's neck. In the Sahara Desert
and Atlas Mountains only sand and sky
and goats and sheep and the donkeys
that seemed willing to carry almost anything.
I remember a river of people, a library of eyes
in the souks where I heard unknown words;
the only one I learned was *shukran,*
when *thank you* seemed enough.
Cats are everywhere in Marrakesh,
weightless and content
along the narrow roads.
The dogs and the roosters
sounded like home.
With my last Moroccan dirhams

I bought a tiny genie lamp,
more magic than prayer,
the way amniotic fluid
is beyond water.
There was a dark,
soft pathway to air.

I give you this splintered, luminous world
you left me. How lucky we are
even though we die.
Perhaps you could have
eaten an apricot or a fragile peach,
no need for fig leaves,
just peach juice running down
a naked chin, a naked neck, a naked chest.
No death. You were thrust into a dying world,
to mother others in a way
you were never mothered.
I always feel for the mother –
that sick man with an assault weapon
who murders all the innocents
had a mother. What is she doing
besides bearing grief & failure?
The mothers of the dead –
all of us breaking.
Aren't we all heading back
to the garden, to the mystery
in the darkness below the earth?

I find myself thirty-seven years into a marriage
& wonder if years are actually days.
I find myself among the 600,000
words in the Oxford English Dictionary,
the way I name the shadows
in that nightly map of sleeplessness.
I find myself in the print
of my fingertips I peeled off
once the Elmer's glue was stiff & clear –
how I'm always lifting layers carefully.
If only I'd saved all those pieces
I might find myself.

I might find myself hiding
under the porch when no one found me.
I might find myself in the gilt-edged
pages under *Sarah*, her laughter at being pregnant,
for one, or maybe under *Eve*, how you keep fluttering
back to the garden and exile as some kind of testament.

I might find myself in the images
I've scrolled through of cecropia moths,
those dark brown & rosy wings,
banded with white stripes, the dark spots
on each wingtip like snake eyes,
each roundness a different story –
the caterpillar who lives for a year
& turns in the slurry of a cocoon
to a moth with no mouth, alive only days

to mate & lay eggs & then starve to death, I guess.
And moths turn into nothing or some into powder
in my cupped hands when I try to save them.

I might find myself if I could transcribe hunger,
listen to those narrow seconds again & again
in a black box I'll never find –
that time you reached for an apple.

                                                To rob an apple tree means there
will be no forgotten apples, that there is
someone who cares about an
apple, doesn't want the good to rot, doesn't want the amazon
to wither, to lose its largeness in
this orbiting world of us.
Eve is the first recycler, she
may have taken what is
a god's, but it was a nourishment, an unwasting, the
same way we open every dark secret
so that life is livable – how what we
name becomes sayable. We cannot do
the burying, can not
let skeletons remain & have
ponderous weight, a borrowed decay to
spread & sink. We all need airing, to learn
the generous currents of wind, the
way emptied clothes dance on a line, the strength

                                    of something invisible that
                            dries & satisfies, how one swallowed bite opens
                                    our eyes to hunger, gives us
                                        desire. There is a beyond
                                    a vastness within ourselves,
                                how we herald each birth,
                                believe each history is
                            a small, important story. It will be our
                tiny account like a container of baby teeth, a birthright
                                    crocheted or just-woven, how we
                            arrive to smell the hedge of jasmine & smile,
                            only that. & perhaps the truth of wildness – our
                        world making itself flecked, shadowed, & mysterious.
                        How we bite into an apple again & again & smile.

Maybe you pictured
the hanging red shine
all night, turning toward
and away from Adam,
who somehow slept.
My boyfriend and I
took slow,
synchronized steps up
the creaking stairs to the attic
to feel naked chest on naked chest.
No god punished us.
We returned fluent

in touch and mouth
and maybe love,
but it didn't last.
I wonder about
your first apple –
was it worth it?

My dive into want
broke some surface
as if I had grown gills
to breathe
in a new world.
Boys became magnets.
The poster of George
holding his guitar
and the one of the Sundance Kid
with his mop of hair.
I was there.
Always taking a bite.

Some animals might be messengers,
not the chipmunks and squirrels
who are just annoying.
But the broad-winged hawk
who circles my sky, lands in the tall pine
tree and calls, insistent and shrill. He is here
for a reason. And the fawn, too,
who keeps returning. She looks
right at me. I've left some apples

on the ground, want her to know
that nothing is forbidden.
A very small part of me
thinks she might unzip
her white-flecked hide
to reveal my mother inside,
a space between worlds
opening, a sweetness.
I can't say
no one wants to die,
but most of us don't.
I'll hang on
until the last
collapsing.

Maybe after this,
we take a break,
let you exhale.
How you are
in *every*thing, *every* le*vel*.

Let's give you a trace
of anonymity,
let you walk out
of the myth
& browse the world,
be easy in the sun

as you skirt the edge,
the ruffled sedge,
pull off the veil of blame
& death, change your script
a bit, apples for the taking,
let you conjure the womb
you wished for.

Let's not let
stories divide our world
again & again.

Let's just love
*ever*yone, imagine
each is a god.

I've been receiving
your postcards –

one postmarked in Santa Fe:
the sky is electric blue with quiet
clouds banked against the endless
mountains

another from the West Coast:
an ocean is an ocean,
water swelling forever

maybe you travel
for a new language. You know
how to pronounce the past
but perhaps want
to learn more
about orchards
farther south.

Across the border:
I'm finding my way
to the ends of the earth

You know about endings,
how we teeter
on the edge of here,
of not here.

You write,
I love a slender moon.

Birth again

Had I given up on you?
Maybe.

Today I walked into my room,
and the morning light fell
on the statue of you
a friend has given me.

Okay, okay.
               I'll come back,
 throw all the pages in the air,
let a fist of autumn wind force me
to lift the unclaimed baggage
I need to find, need to unpack.

              It's as if you want me
to tell everyone that women are more hungry
than men, that we carry the yoke of creating,
and when we are growing something inside of us,
we need more sustenance, and when we are nursing,
there are two of us.

Aren't we always hungry?

Our hips need heft for holding.

Is that why you are in my room
saying, *I ate the fucking apple
because I was fucking hungry!*

That push from behind
to get up a steepness –
that's you right now.

The row of newborn clothes
in a cleaned closet lingers.
My daughter's new address
of ready-or-not, of folded blankets
to unfold, of touch.
I used to believe my hands
could calm my children's cries.
And now I have become friends
with yeast – making something come alive
with warm water and kneading
as if I am a god, albeit a minor one.
I don't understand Reiki. Why not touch?
And yet I do believe in the energy
of between – look how magnets pull.
Think about the moon
tied to us, and us tethered to a star.
It takes about eight minutes
for the sun's light to reach us,
the warmth when a cloud shifts with wind.
93,000,000 miles of only space.
I knew a woman who couldn't bear
the distance: her daughter on another continent
for a semester, how she lay on the floor

and wept, needed medication.
It's hard to cut the cord,
let them live beyond us.
In the rubble of re-creation,
we can remake ourselves
as mothers – the quiet rhyme
of forgiveness and future.

Sometimes I forget
the *Odyssey* was a song

forgive me –
I need to speak about Penelope
her silent victories of unweaving
hearing her son sneeze
and knowing about signs

she and I witness them
the broad-winged hawk   its plaintive whistle
my mother returning to welcome
a great-granddaughter to this Earth

there are many worlds
Ithaka inside me –
my mother, and now
the sweet new life

the next chapter –
grandmother   holding forever
on the edge   ready to jump

I don't know where
commas go or periods –
exclamation everywhere!

a melody rises in the blood
rhyme in the marrow – untouched
and touching everything

I hold my granddaughter
her weight a love letter
I didn't know I'd receive
a prayer I hadn't prayed

even the birds stop singing
to hear her breathe

Maybe we're moving too fast,
traveling 600,000 miles an hour

around a star. Why isn't everything
a blur? Or maybe it is.

It's hard to stand still,
the way Rilke must have

in front of the archaic torso
of Apollo, the remnant of sculpture

where light pulsed from a stone.
My granddaughter is unbruised

and suffused with all good.
A recognition.

Us at our best.
In a world

where we can
become our worst.

Let's remember
how we enter the world.

Perfect. Needing
to be held.

Where everything is wholly
holy, where we have transparent
skin & the liminal is not wedged
between what was & what will be.
There are no relics, nothing calcified.
We are open envelopes, our sadnesses
a mural we wear. Our aches, unfurled
wings. It is a raw world. Unhusked.
Tears flow, but no one wants
to leave. Everywhere unfenced,
no locked gate to any garden.
Dawn is breaking, no one
breaking inside, no one
unseen.

She might remember me,
by which I mean,
this is how we are reborn,
our little cluster of cells
contained by the skin will end,
but I'm imagining one day
she'll tell her daughter
about a grandmother
who looked in her eyes
like she was the sun,
that beautiful,
to her grandmother,
who made her feel
that everything
was pulled toward her.

NOTES:

Italicized words on page 49 are Lucille Clifton's from my favorite poem, "blessing the boats." The right-aligned piece on pages 66 & 67 is a Golden Shovel of "female" by Lucille Clifton.

My gratitude extends to a village of poets who have generously read my work and made it better: Wendy Drexler, Margot Wizansky, Steve Nickman, Xiaoly Li, Connemara Wadsworth, Anastasia Vassos, Laura Foley, Peggy Brightman, Jill Herrick-Lee, Deb Franzoni, Jon Escher, Lynne Byler, Joanne Durham, Jayne Marek, Eileen Cleary, Christine Jones, Frances Donovan, Anna V. Q. Voss, Jennifer Martelli, Melissa McKinstry, Judith Fox, Elizabeth Tan, and Carol Young. To my mentors: Barbara Helfgott Hyatt, Ellen Bass, Frank X. Gaspar, Marie Howe, Traci Brimhall, Kelli Russell Agodon, Mark Doty, Rick Barot, and Kim Addonizio. Thank you, Michael McInnis and Annie Pluto for believing in this book. To my sisters, too. And of course, to my children, Abby and David, and the lovely people, Paul and Emily, they have married. And to Ellie, who moves us into a new generation and gives me hope and whose initials are EVE. And mostly to you, Ben.

ABOUT THE AUTHOR

After decades in the classroom, Sarah Dickenson Snyder carves in stone, sculls on the Connecticut River, and rides her bike. Travel opens her eyes. She has five poetry collections: *The Human Contract* (2017), *Notes from a Nomad* (nominated for the Massachusetts Book Awards 2018), *With a Polaroid Camera* (2019), and *Now These Three Remain* (nominated for the Massachusetts Book Awards 2023). Several poems have been nominated for Best of Net and Pushcart Prizes. Work is in *Rattle*, *Verse Daily*, and *RHINO*. sarahdickensonsnyder.com

42° 19' 47.9" N · 70° 56' 43.9" W

Nixes Mate is a navigational hazard in Boston Harbor used during the colonial period to gibbet and hang pirates and mutineers.

Nixes Mate Books features small-batch artisanal literature, created by writers who use all 26 letters of the alphabet and then some, honing their craft the time-honored way: one line at a time.

nixesmate.pub

www.ingramcontent.com/pod-product-compliance
Lightning Source LLC
LaVergne TN
LVHW072000080526
838202LV00064B/6805